READING POWER

Writing in the Ancient World

WRITING IN ANCIENT EGYPT

JIL FINE

The Rosen Publishing Group's
PowerKids Press™
New York

Published in 2003 by The Rosen Publishing Group, Inc.
29 East 21st Street, New York, NY 10010

First Edition

Book Design: Michael DeLisio

Photo Credits: Cover, p. 13 © Sandro Vannini/Corbis; pp. 4–5 © Ben Mangor/SuperStock; pp. 4, (inset), 6 Michael DeLisio; p. 7 © Hari D. Shourie/SuperStock; p. 8 Scala/Art Resource, NY; p. 9 © H.M. Herget/National Geographic Image Collection; pp. 10–11 © SuperStock; pp. 10 (inset), 12 The British Museum, London; p.14 © Peter Johnson/ Corbis; p. 15 © Giraudon/Art Resource, NY; pp. 16, 19 © Bettman/ Corbis; p. 17 Duke University, Rare Book, Manuscript and Special Collections Library; p. 20 Art Resource, NY; p. 21 © Roger Ressmeyer/ Corbis

Library of Congress Cataloging-in-Publication Data

Fine, Jil.
Writing in ancient Egypt / Jil Fine.
    p. cm. — (Writing in the ancient world)
Includes bibliographical references and index.
ISBN 0-8239-6506-6 (library binding)
1. Egyptian language—Writing. I. Title. II. Series.
PJ1051 .F56 2003
493'.111—dc21
                                2002000503

Contents

ANCIENT EGYPT

Ancient Egyptians lived along the Nile River about 5,000 years ago. Much of the land was desert. The Egyptians depended on the river for farming and travel. They built huge pyramids, created a 365-day calendar, and started their own way of writing.

Mediterranean Sea

EGYPT

Red Sea

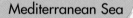

Nile River

The ancient Egyptians often wrote about their history and religion on the walls of their buildings.

HIEROGLYPHICS

The Egyptians invented a system of writing called hieroglyphics. Hieroglyphs were pictures that stood for objects, sounds, or ideas. Many pictures could have more than one meaning. Hieroglyphs could also spell a word by using a picture for the sound of each syllable. There were more than 700 different hieroglyphic pictures in ancient Egyptian writing.

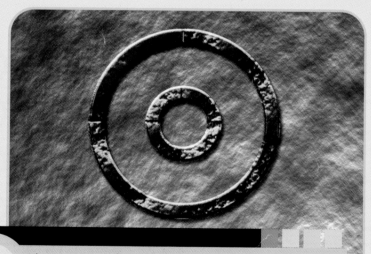

The picture of a circle inside another circle could stand for the sun. It could also mean "day," since the sun comes up during the day.

Ancient Egyptian hieroglyphics were usually written from right to left, but sometimes the pictures could be placed from top to bottom or left to right.

Very few people in ancient Egypt knew how to read or write. People who learned to read and write were called scribes. They went to special scribe schools to learn how to read and write hieroglyphic pictures. Being a scribe was one of the most important and respected jobs in ancient Egypt.

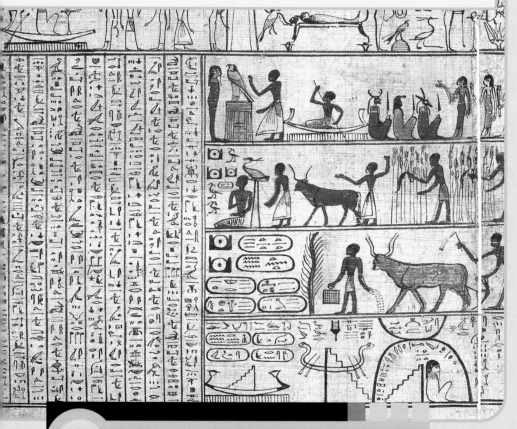

An Egyptian scribe wrote this to tell about life in ancient Egypt.

A person had to go to school for four or five years in order to become a scribe.

Hieroglyphs were used mainly on monuments and temple walls. They were cut in stone or painted on metal or wood. Hammers and sharp tools were used to cut hieroglyphs into stone.

▶ *These tools were used to cut hieroglyphics into stone walls.*

Hieroglyphic *means* "sacred carving."

HIERATIC WRITING

The ancient Egyptians also invented hieratic writing. Hieratic signs were easier and faster to write than hieroglyphic signs. They were written with reed pens and ink on smooth surfaces.

Ancient Egyptians often used the ashes of burnt wood to make ink. The ink was put into inkwells such as these.

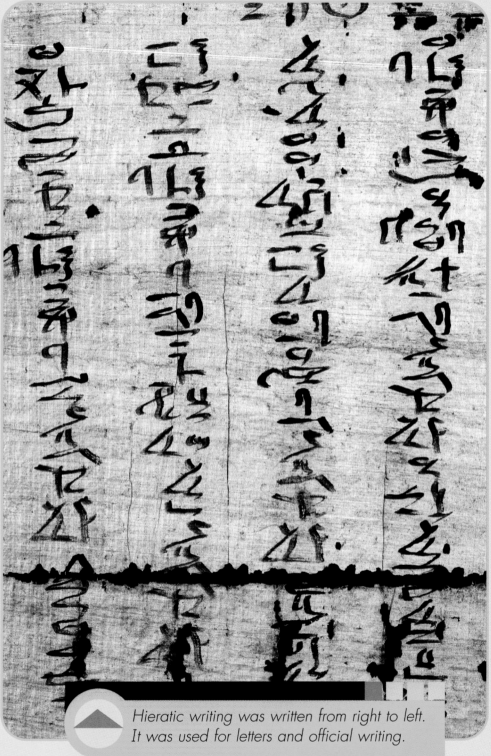

Hieratic writing was written from right to left. It was used for letters and official writing.

Ancient Egyptians used papyrus, a tall water plant, to invent the world's first paper. They flattened the papyrus into thin, smooth scrolls. Reeds, or tall grass, were used to make pens. Scribes wrote mostly in black and red ink.

Papyrus grows along the banks of the Nile River.

▶ The longest known Egyptian scroll is 135 feet long.

The word paper comes from the word papyrus.

DEMOTIC WRITING

Demotic writing, an even faster form of writing than hieratic, was created in 660 B.C. This writing was used by the government and businesses. It was also used for writing stories. After demotic writing was invented, hieratic writing was mainly used for religious writing.

CHECK IT OUT

The ancient Egyptians had a very large library in the city of Alexandria. It held more than 400,000 papyrus scrolls on subjects such as astronomy and geography.

17

LOST AND FOUND

Alexander the Great, a Greek king, took control of Egypt in 332 B.C. The Greek alphabet and language then started to replace the Egyptian writing. Some Egyptians still wrote in hieroglyphics until about 400 A.D. After hieroglyphics were no longer used, people forgot how to read them.

Although Alexander the Great (left, in picture) died at the young age of thirty-three, he changed the history of the world by taking over many countries, including Egypt.

19

In 1799, the Rosetta Stone was found in Egypt. It helped people to read and understand ancient Egyptian writing.

The Rosetta Stone shows the three writings that were used in ancient Egypt: hieroglyphic, demotic, and ancient Greek. The words on the Rosetta Stone honor an Egyptian king.

Each time we read ancient Egyptian writing we learn new things about this society. Who knows what clues about the life of these interesting people still lay buried!

The ancient Egyptians buried their dead leaders in tall pyramids in the desert.

Glossary

cursive (**kehr**-sihv) writing with flowing and joined letters

demotic (**dih**-ma-tihk) a simple form of hieratic writing; for business, government, and everyday uses

hieratic (**hy**-ra-tihk) a cursive form of hieroglyphic writing

hieroglyphics (**hy**-ruh-glih-fihks) a writing system that uses pictures as signs

hieroglyphs (**hy**-ruh-gliphs) ancient Egyptian pictures that stand for a word, an idea, or a sound

papyrus (puh-**py**-ruhs) a tall water plant that grows in the Nile valley

pyramids (**pihr**-uh-mihdz) large buildings in which ancient Egyptians buried their kings

scribe (**skryb**) someone who knew how to read and write in ancient Egypt

scroll (**skrohl**) a roll of papyrus sheets used for writing

syllable (**sihl**-uh-buhl) a letter or group of letters in a word that are said together

Resources

Books

Eyewitness: Ancient Egypt
by George Hart
Dorling Kindersley Publishing (2000)

The Riddle of the Rosetta Stone:
Key to Ancient Egypt
by James Cross Giblin
HarperCollins Children's Books (1996)

Web Sites

Due to the changing nature of Internet links, PowerKids Press has developed an on-line list of Web sites related to the subjects of this book. This site is updated regularly. Please use this link to access the list:

http://www.powerkidslinks.com/waw/aneg/

Index

Word Count: 422

Note to Librarians, Teachers, and Parents

If reading is a challenge, Reading Power is a solution! Reading Power is perfect for readers who want high-interest subject matter at an accessible reading level. These fact-filled, photo-illustrated books are designed for readers who want straightforward vocabulary, engaging topics, and a manageable reading experience. With clear picture/text correspondence, leveled Reading Power books put the reader in charge. Now readers have the power to get the information they want and the skills they need in a user-friendly format.